A DAY IN THE CITY

by Polly Peterson
illustrated by Nancy Coffelt

Harcourt

Orlando   Boston   Dallas   Chicago   San Diego

Visit *The Learning Site!*
www.harcourtschool.com

The city is an exciting place. There is so much to see and do. Would you like to find out what's here? Let's go!

Let's start right here in front of this apartment building. It is a big building. Many families live here. Do you live in an apartment, too?

We can walk from here to the subway.
First we have to cross this busy street. Cars
and trucks are zooming past!

Let's stay on the sidewalk. We will walk to the traffic light. That is a safe place to cross. Be sure to wait until the sign says, **WALK**.

The subway train is underground. We need to go down a long stairway to get there. There are lots of people waiting for the train.

The subway goes fast! It goes through
dark tunnels. We can't see the city this way!
That's okay. We'll get off at the next stop.

Here we are in the city center. The
buildings are very tall! Some of them seem
to touch the sky. We call them skyscrapers.

Let's go to the top of one of the
skyscrapers. First, we need to buy a ticket.
Then, we'll go up in an elevator.

The views from up here are great! We can
see the city below. Buildings and streets go
on and on in every direction.

Can you see the river? Cars are crossing the river on bridges. Can you see the park? It has lots of trees and a lake. There is a museum in the park, too. Let's go!

This sidewalk leads to the park. We walk
past people who are eating at a restaurant.
We walk past lots of stores.

It's a beautiful day in the park. We can buy
lunch here. Let's sit on a park bench to eat
our lunch. Then we will go to the museum.

The museum is very big. There are lots of things to look at. There are lots of things to learn. Let's follow the signs to the dinosaur exhibit.

The dinosaur skeletons are huge! It's fun to learn about dinosaurs. We can learn about many other animals here, too.

Exploring the museum is fun, but now it's getting late. Our day in the city is almost over. There is so much more to see and do! We'll have to come back another day.